May these pages hold your intimate moments of

reflections, prayers, and hallmark of dreams realized...

Joelle Marie André Kabamba
AUTHOR

The Unexpected Gift Journal
Copyright © 2021 by Joëlle Marie-André Kabamba
First Published in Australia by Space Between Publications

Space Between Publications
ParcelLocker 1021607003
50FlemingtonRoad
ParkvilleVIC3052
www.spacebetweenpublications.com

Designed by Annie K Kabamba
Model Armelle Ndonat Heville
ISBN 978-0-6488656-0-5
Typesetting services by **Self-PublishingLab.com**

Coming up to them at that very moment, she gave thanks to God and spoke about the child to all who were looking forward to the redemption of Jerusalem.

Lk 2:38

Blessed is she who has believed that the Lord would fulfill his promises to her!
Lk 1:45

In the beginning was the word, and the word was with God, and the Word was God. He was with God in the beginning. Through him all things were made; without him nothing was made that has been made.

John 1:1-3

The angel went to her and said, "Greetings, you who are highly favoured! The Lord is with you".

Lk 1:28

In him was life, and life was the light of all mankind. The light shines in the darkness, and the darkness has not overcome it.

John 1:4-5

For God so loved the world that he gave his one and only Son, that whoever believes in him shall not perish but have eternal life.

John 3:16

...but a woman who fears the Lord is to be praised.
Pr 31:30

But God demonstrates his own love for us in this: While we were still sinners, Christ died for us.

Romans 5:8

"The Lord has done this for me," she said. "In these days he has shown his favour and taken away my disgrace among the people."
Lk 1:25

Whoever believes in the Son has eternal life, but whoever rejects the Son will not see life, for God's wrath remains on them.

John 3:36

I want to know Christ ~ yes, to know the power of his resurrection and participation in his sufferings, becoming like him in his death.

Phil 3:10